MYSTERIES IN HISTORY

What Happened to Pompeii?

Solving the Mysteries of the Past

Charlie Samuels

Cavendish
Square
New York

Published in 2018 by Cavendish Square Publishing, LLC
243 5th Avenue, Suite 136 New York, NY 10016

Website: cavendishsq.com

© 2018 Brown Bear Books Ltd

Cataloging-in-Publication Data

Names: Samuels, Charlie.
Title: What happened to Pompeii? / Charlie Samuels.
Description: New York : Cavendish Square Publishing, 2018. | Series: Mysteries in history: solving the mysteries of the past
| Includes index.
Identifiers: ISBN 9781502628022 (library bound) | ISBN 9781502628039 (ebook)
Subjects: LCSH: Pompeii (Extinct city)--Juvenile literature. | Vesuvius (Italy)--Eruption, 79--Juvenile literature.
Classification: LCC DG70.P7 S265 2018 | DDC 937'.72568--dc23

For Brown Bear Books Ltd:
Managing Editor: Tim Cooke
Designer: Lynne Lennon
Editorial Director: Lindsey Lowe
Design Manager: Keith Davis
Children's Publisher: Anne O'Daly
Picture Manager: Sophie Mortimer

Contents

Who Found the Buried City?

The Roman city of Pompeii, and its neighbor, Herculaneum, had been buried and forgotten for centuries. Then, in the early 1700s, their dramatic stories were rediscovered.

In the early 1700s, workers were digging a well near the Bay of Naples in southern Italy. Above them rose the great volcano, Mount Vesuvius. The workers found some old stones. As they cleared the earth away, they realized

The cone-shaped Mount Vesuvius rises behind the ruins of Pompeii.

that the "stones" were statues of women. The women wore the kind of clothes that were once worn by the ancient Romans. What were they doing in the Naples countryside?

Naples

Pompeii

Bay of Naples

The ruins at Pompeii give a clear idea of what a Roman town would have looked like.

Key Clue

In 1734, Naples and the countryside around it came under the control of a new king, Charles VII. He heard about the discovery of the mysterious statues and sent soldiers to look for more old objects. He hoped to be able to sell anything they found to art collectors. His soldiers soon found more old statues. They also uncovered the first clue to help identify what they might be. One of the pieces of stone was carved with letters. When an expert studied the writing, he recognized it as being Latin. Latin was the language used by the ancient Romans. The fragment of text read "the theater of Herculaneum."

SCIENCE SOLVES IT

Digging Up Pompeii

Johann Winckelmann, a German art historian and archaeologist, is sometimes known as the "Father of **Archaeology**." He was interested in **excavating** ancient sites. When he visited Pompeii in 1760, Winckelmann did not think digging up the ancient city would be worthwhile. If Pompeii and Herculaneum had been buried by volcanic **lava**, he thought, both cities would have been crushed by the weight so nothing would be left to be discovered.

Winckelmann studied cameos, or brooches, found in other Roman cities.

Historians recognized the name. Accounts left by ancient Roman writers described how the town of Herculaneum had once stood near the foot of Mount Vesuvius. Herculaneum had been buried by lava after an **eruption** of Vesuvius in 79 CE. The buried statues had once stood in a city that had been buried for more than 1,500 years. If this was the site of Herculaneum, historians knew there would be other valuable ruins to be uncovered.

The stories about the destruction of Herculaneum said that another city had been destroyed at the same time. This was Pompeii. In 1748, King Charles sent his soldiers back to Herculaneum to look for this second site. They heard that local people had discovered old **artifacts** at a site about 12.5 miles (20 km) down the coast from Mount Vesuvius.

The ancient Romans stored foods and liquids in these clay urns.

7

One Mystery Solved

The soil at the new site was easier to dig than at Herculaneum. The soldiers quickly found buried stone walls and some human bones. The soldiers took whatever they thought would have value among art collectors. No one was certain, however, that this was a second buried city.

Although the soldiers found more statues and other old objects, there was no proof that it was the city of Pompeii. The mystery was solved 15 years later. In 1763, diggers at the site found the evidence they had been looking for. A Latin sign carved into a wall revealed that this was indeed the once-thriving Roman town of Pompeii.

ANCIENT SECRETS

A Dead Language

Some ancient languages are difficult to read. Luckily for experts at Pompeii and Herculaneum, the Romans used Latin. Latin is referred to as a dead, or no longer spoken, language, but it is the basis of languages such as Italian and Spanish. Latin has been taught in Europe for centuries. That made it possible to read the ancient inscriptions on the stones at Pompeii.

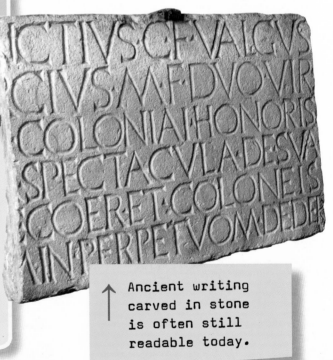

↑ Ancient writing carved in stone is often still readable today.

↑ Diggers found red paint on walls throughout Pompeii.

Treasure Hunting

Today, if an ancient site is discovered almost anywhere in the world, it is protected until archeologists can investigate the remains. In the past, however, few people were concerned about preserving such sites. For nearly 200 years following their discovery, the sites at Herculaneum and Pompeii were used as sources of valuable objects to sell. Treasure hunters even used gunpowder to blow apart the ruins to reach more objects.

By the middle of the 19th century, some people began to suggest that it was wrong to destroy ancient ruins and steal their treasures. Experts thought that saving and studying the ruins of these

In ancient Roman times, wealthy people's homes often had a courtyard with a pool. The pool's water helped to cool the air.

ancient towns would help them to learn more about ancient civlizations. At the time, many details about everyday life in ancient Rome were still a mystery. Archeologists thought that Pompeii and Herculaneum might reveal valuable information.

The Past Revealed

Giuseppe Fiorelli was an archeologist who worked for the Italian government. He took charge of the site at Pompeii in 1860. Fiorelli immediately stopped any further **looting** of artifacts from the site. He also made ambitious plans to excavate the whole Roman city. Dividing the area into nine numbered sections, he ordered his work crews to begin the **methodical** clearing of soil and rubble from the site. Slowly, the workers began to expose buildings, then streets, and eventually whole neighborhoods emerged.

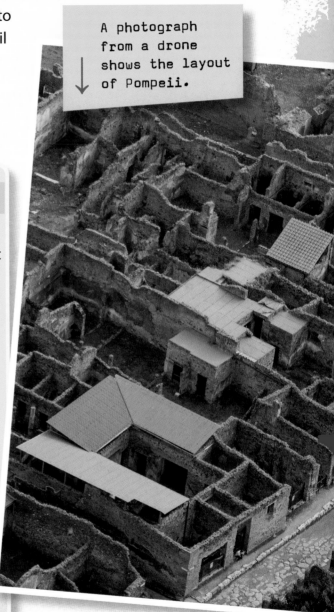

A photograph from a drone shows the layout of Pompeii.

SCIENCE SOLVES IT

Technology at Work

Modern archeologists use the latest technology. As at Pompeii, many archeological finds in the past were made by accident. However, modern techniques allow archeologists to see what lies beneath the ground before they start digging. Light Detection and Ranging (LiDAR) technology creates 3-D images of whatever lie in the soil. At Pompeii, ground-penetrating **radar** has shown what might be hidden in spaces that have not yet been excavated. Meanwhile, **drones** fitted with cameras can give a bird's-eye view of sites.

A modern-day team of archaeologists excavate a building at Pompeii.

What Lay Buried?

The site at Pompeii was far larger than anyone had realized. Even today, around two-fifths of Pompeii are still buried, after nearly 150 years of archaeological work at the site. As Fiorelli's workers cleared walls and streets, he made sure that they left artifacts exactly where they found them. Fiorelli realized that the location of objects was nearly as important as the objects themselves. Where things were found helped archaeologists to figure out exactly what had happened on the day Mount Vesuvius erupted. They found dishes of olives on tables and loaves of bread that might have come fresh from the bakery.

For experts, such clues were fascinating. There had never been such an insight into Roman life. But would they be able to piece together a picture of how the citizens of Pompeii and Herculaneum had lived and died? What could they discover about the terrible tragedy that had destroyed two great cities? And what would they find out about the fate of the people who had lived there?

ANCIENT SECRETS

Is There More to Discover?
Today, student archaeologists from around the world are trained on the excavations at Pompeii and Herculaneum. Although nearly half of Pompeii has been excavated, only a few streets of Herculaneum have been cleared. Many of that city's secrets still lay hidden in Mount Vesuvius's rubble and ash.

Excavation revealed decorations inside one Pompeiian home.

What Happened?

What would it be like to live through a volcanic eruption? Experts at Pompeii and Herculaneum have revealed many facts about the horrifying events of August 24, 79 CE.

Experts have unraveled the mystery of how the citizens of the two towns panicked and tried to escape. The most revealing and most grisly sources of information is the remains of the people themselves. In other volcanic disasters, the super-hot lava destroys all traces of victims, even their bones.

Victims of Mount Vesuvius's eruption lay throughout Pompeii.

This family took shelter beside a wall as they tried to escape.

At Pompeii, however, the way in which people died left a unique record. Herculaneum has equally grim evidence of its inhabitants' last moments.

Spaces in the Rock

While Giuseppe Fiorelli's workers cleared Pompeii in the 1860s, they came across what seemed to be empty spaces in the ground. They wondered what could have caused these holes. Some of the shapes looked almost human. Fiorelli figured out that the spaces must have been created by the bodies of people who had died. The volcanic ash buried their bodies as it fell from the sky. Over centuries the ash compressed and formed **pumice**, a kind of porous rock.

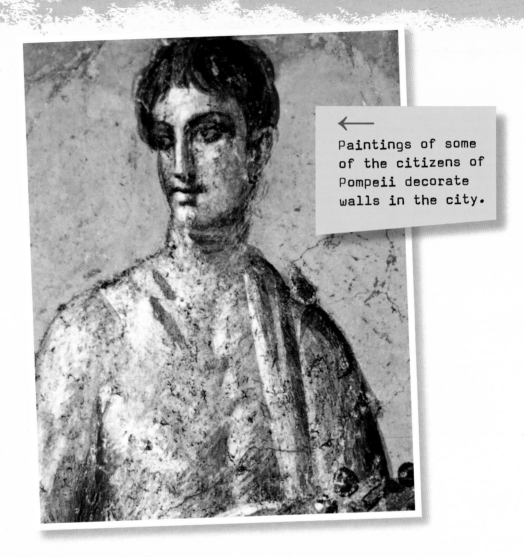

Paintings of some of the citizens of Pompeii decorate walls in the city.

The Bodies of Pompeii

To test his theory, Fiorelli mixed up some liquid plaster. He poured the plaster into one of the mysterious spaces in the rock until the space was full. When the plaster had hardened, the archaeologists cleared away the covering of stone. The plaster cast revealed the shape of a terrified victim of the volcano. Fiorelli figured out that, over decades and centuries, the bodies buried under the ash had decayed. Some bodies had crumbled away until only bones were left. Then some of the bones had crumbled away, too.

The ash around the bodies had hardened into rock, which then and preserved the shape of the original body. With this mystery solved, archaeologists were able to use the plaster technique to preserve the shapes of hundreds of Pompeiian citizens who had died.

The remains of a Minoan palace at Knossos on Crete that was destroyed by the eruption of Thera.
↓

IN CONTEXT

Volcanic Disaster

Pompeii and Herculaneum were not the only cities that fell victim to volcanic eruptions in the ancient world. In around 1600 BCE, Thera erupted on the Greek island of Santorini. It destroyed the Minoan civilization on the nearby island of Crete. **Tsunamis** caused by the eruption devastated Crete. Ash hung in the sky for years, causing harvests to fail. Minoan culture crumbled. The region took centuries to recover.

Tale of the Skeletons

For years, experts thought most residents managed to flee from Herculaneum. Human remains were only found there in 1980. Archeologists found 300 skeletons huddled together. They had tried to flee, but had only reached the coastline when a wave of gas and ash killed them. That showed that the city's fate was different from the gradual rain of ash that fell on Pompeii.

It is rare to find Roman bones. The dead were usually burned.

Whole families were buried together. Servants were buried as they tried to carry away their employers' possessions. Cats and dogs died where they were abandoned as their owners fled.

A New Mystery

The next mystery to be solved was why all these victims had failed to escape Mount Vesuvius's eruption. Experts have put together the story of what they think may have happened. Some written accounts of the disaster that have survived helped the experts understand the timeline of that day. They also studied the precise locations where the bodies were found inside the cities.

Signs of Disaster

In 79 CE, Mount Vesuvius had been **dormant** for hundreds of years. Large towns had grown in the shadow of the volcano. There was no reason for the people living there to expect things to change. They did not recognize the warning signs.

The first signs of the disaster came days before Mount Vesuvius erupted. The ground began to shake regularly. There had been earthquakes in the region before. Some people moved away for safety. But most citizens of Pompeii did not realize how serious the danger was. They carried on with their daily lives.

Smoke rising from an active volcano may be a sign of a coming eruption.

This family dog was abandoned and died in the ash at Pompeii.

Mount Vesuvius Erupts

Early on the morning of August 24, Mount Vesuvius sent a column of smoke and ash into the sky. More people decided to leave town. A few hours later, around 1:00 p.m., the volcano erupted with a huge roar. A jet of red-hot rock, ash, and smoke shot some 17 miles (27 km) into the air. As rocks and ash from this cloud started to fall on Pompeii, people grabbed what they could and left town. As the ash piled up, it began to crush buildings. Some people died when wooden roofs fell under the weight. Others were killed by falling rocks. Most people, however, managed to escape over the next few hours.

Too Late!

Those who hesitated were not so lucky. About 2,000 people stayed in the city. No one knows why they stayed, although there are many theories. Perhaps they still did not understand the danger they were in. They may have chosen to stay behind to guard their homes or businesses from looters. Perhaps they were searching for relatives or friends.

SCIENCE SOLVES IT

What Do Bones Tell Us?
The skeletons at Herculaneum were valuable for archaeologists. The length of arm and leg bones give clues about how tall a person was. Bones can also reveal a person's age when they died, any diseases they had, and their usual diet. At Herculaneum, the bones had a high lead content. The Romans did not know that lead is poisonous. They drank wine from lead goblets.

This computer-generated image of a victim's face was created using measurements taken from a skull at Herculaneum.

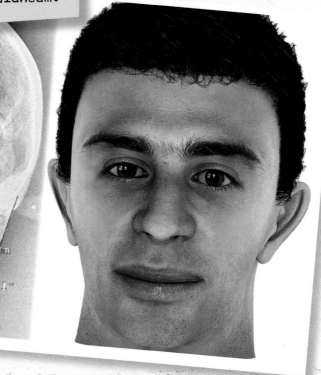

It is possible that they were sick and unable to move easily. Or perhaps they were trying to save their possessions. Eventually, however, it was too late. There was so much ash in the streets that people were stuck. There was no escape.

Death Comes in an Instant

In Herculaneum, the story was very different. There, the only remains to have been found are bones. When Mount Vesuvius erupted, the wind blew the smoke and ash toward Pompeii. But that did not mean that Herculaneum had escaped disaster. At around 1:00 a.m., a column of poisonous gases, rocks, and pumice shot out from the side of the volcano toward Herculaneum.

Traveling at up to 100 miles per hour (160 kmh), the wave of gas and rock took just four minutes to swamp the town. Some people rushed towad the sea to try to escape by boat. They died on the shore. Having struck the city, the **pyroclastic flow** continued onto the Bay of Naples. As it entered the water, the sea started to boil.

A Last Cloud

This was not the end of Mount Vesuvius's eruptions. The volcano began to spew boiling lava. The lava rushed downhill toward Herculaneum, submerging the city until it was completely hidden from sight. Meanwhile, a final cloud of gas and ash shot out of the volcano and headed toward Pompeii. The few people left in the city who had been lucky enough to survive the earlier eruptions died instantly.

Lava flowed down the side of Mount Vesuvius and submerged Herculaneum.

What Were the Cities Like?

Many of the mysteries about what life was like in Pompeii have now been answered. But Herculaneum still holds many secrets.

Herculaneum has been only partly excavated because the modern city of Ercolano has been built directly on top of parts of the Roman city. Historians and politicians have talked about digging up parts of the newer town in order to discover more about the ancient town.

The buildings of Ercolano rise above the ruins of Herculaneum.

For now, experts have agreed to stop further excavations at Herculaneum. The technology does not yet exist that would allow them to excavate the old city without destroying Ercolano. Instead, archaeologists have learned everything they can from the artifacts and buildings at the site throughout the last 200 years. Ancient Roman writings inform us that Herculaneum was a small suburb outside a larger city known as Neapolis (modern-day Naples). Fishing was its most important industry, but the town also had craftsmen and workshops. Historians think that it was more of an industrial center than its richer neighbor, Pompeii.

This temple in Pompeii was dedicated to the god Jupiter.

Frozen in Time

While excavation at Herculaneum has stopped, experts are learning more and more about life in Pompeii. When the stone and ash rained down on the town in 79 CE, the blanket of volcanic debris acted like a huge seal. It preserved everything beneath it until archeologists began methodical excavations in the late 1800s.

Pompeii was the larger of the two cities. It was also wealthier.

IN CONTEXT

Herculaneum vs. Pompeii

Herculaneum was much smaller in area and population than its neighbor. It was only about a quarter or a third of the size of Pompeii, which covers around 163 acres (66 hectares). Pompeii's population was between 12,000 and 15,000, while Herculaneum probably had no more than 5,000 inhabitants. Pompeii was also a wealthier town than its neighbor.

The Forum at Pompeii was home to temples and market stalls.

Ancient reports said that all Roman cities and towns were laid out in the same way, so experts knew what they were looking for. There was a large square called the **forum**. It featured an open-air marketplace and was also home to public buildings and temples. The forum was surrounded by streets laid out in a regular grid pattern consisting of blocks of houses, stores, and workshops.

The evidence suggests that Pompeii was a much wealthier city than Herculaneum. However, both cities had the same public buildings: baths, theaters, temples, and markets.

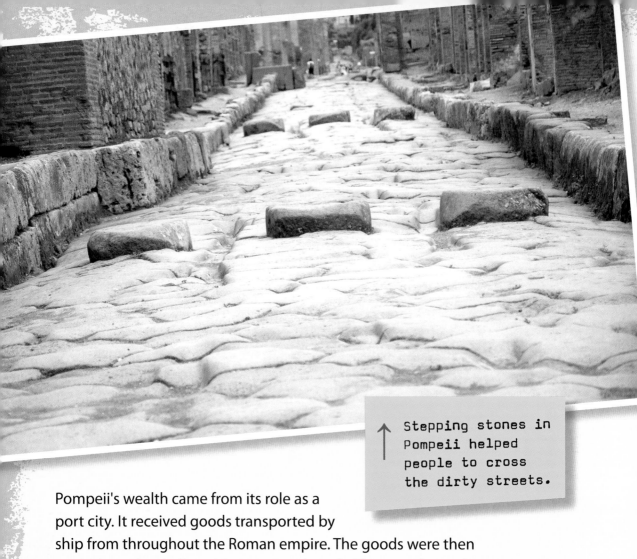

↑ Stepping stones in Pompeii helped people to cross the dirty streets.

Pompeii's wealth came from its role as a port city. It received goods transported by ship from throughout the Roman empire. The goods were then carried to other Italian cities on paved roads. The straight roads allowed goods to be transported quickly.

Confirming the Accounts

The forum was a large, open rectangular-shaped space at the center of Pompeii. Around the forum were covered **galleries** that were used as stores by merchants. The forum was also home to a basilica. This was a large building that served as a court of law or as another place for public meetings. The basilica was the most important building in Pompeii.

Because Pompeii was a wealthy town, its inhabitants could pay for statues to be put up in the forum. Around 40 statues have been discovered there so far. The statues show different gods and Roman emperors. They also portray leading citizens from the town. Another building in the forum was the Temple of Jupiter. The temple honored Jupiter, who was thought to be the father of all the Roman gods.

IN CONTEXT

An Extensive Empire

At its peak in around 117 CE, the Roman Empire stretched all the way across Europe, and from Britain in the north to Egypt in the south. The Romans linked the empire with a network of straight roads. Wherever they went, the Romans built cities modeled on Rome. The cities were laid out on a grid pattern and had the same buildings: bathhouses, temples, and a forum.

Roman engineers built straight roads like this across the entirety of the Roman Empire.

↑ These statues surrounded part of Pompeii's public bathhouse.

Signs of Wealth

As archaeologists uncovered Pompeii, its wealthy past was revealed. One clue was the main shopping street, known as the "street of plenty." The number and variety of stores suggest that there must have been many rich customers in the town. Pompeiians could buy anything they wanted! The stores sold exotic goods imported from as far away as India and China. The street itself had gutters to carry away dirty water and rain. There were also raised stepping stones in order to prevent people from getting their feet dirty as they crossed the street.

Pompeii also had many fountains with clean drinking water. The water was carried from the countryside to Pompeii, Herculaneum, and other cities by an **aqueduct** named for the Emperor Augustus, the Aqua Augusta. The aqueduct covered over 87 miles (140 km). Inside Pompeii, the water was distributed to bathhouses, private homes, and fountains throughout the city. It was carried by a network of specially built underground pipes.

A system of heating pipes and water pools controlled the temperature in bathhouses like this.

Sociable Bathing

Water was important to the Romans. They believed in keeping clean. Bathing in Roman times was a social event. People met their friends in the baths and chatted while they got clean. Three public bathhouses have been found in Pompeii. Each bathhouse had a series of rooms, with pools ranging from very cold to very hot. Bathers went from one room to another. The hot room (*caldarium*) was heated by steam that came through the floor and walls. It helped people sweat out dirt from the skin. They then scraped the dirt off using oil and a special scraper.

↑ The theater at Pompeii could seat thousands of spectators.

ANCIENT SECRETS

A Changing Town

Pompeii changed over time. In the late 1800s the archeologist August Mau identified that some buildings were much older than others. The oldest buildings, near the Forum, dated back to 300 BCE. The most recent changes had come in 62 CE, when a powerful earthquake struck the city. Many wealthier residents left Pompeii. Their homes became workshops for traders and craftsmen. The city continued to flourish until the eruption seventeen years later.

↑ This wall painting in Pompeii shows the goddess Venus lying in a seashell.

After the hot room they visited a room of medium heat (*tepidarium*), and a room with a cold bath (*frigidarium*). Most people used the public baths. Only wealthy people had a bathroom in their home. At Pompeii, bathing must have been popular. Archeologists discovered that a fourth bathhouse was in the process of being built when disaster struck.

A Trip to the Theater

Going to the theater was another important social event for the Romans. Pompeii's **amphitheater** was so large it could seat most of the town's population. The amphitheater did not only stage plays. **Gladiator** fights were also held there.

The Gardens of Pompeii

About a third of homes in Pompeii had gardens. Even smaller homes had strips of land with plants. Some gardens grew vegetables, but others grew flowers or shrubs. In the 1960s and 1970s, garden expert Wilhelmina Jashemski studied the gardens of Pompeii. She took plaster casts of holes left by roots in the soil to find out what plants made them. She also studied the contours of the soil, so she could identify where flower beds once stood.

City Buildings

What else have the excavations revealed? The citizens of Pompeii liked to drink alcohol with each other. There were more than 100 bars in the town. When citizens had finished socializing, or had finished shopping, they headed home.

Experts have not been able to learn much about homes in Herculaneum. It is likely that they

A stream ran through this garden to help keep it cool.

were similar to those in Pompeii. Magnificent **villas** once stood on the hills outside Pompeii. They often had 50 or more rooms and were lived in by wealthy Roman families. It seems that Pompeii was used as a seaside getaway where affluent Romans could enjoy the cooling sea breezes during the hot Italian summer.

Homes in the city center ranged from large villas with private gardens or courtyards to small one-room apartments. We even know what plants grew in Pompeii's gardens because experts have been able to identify them during excavation work. One garden had so many fragrant plants that archeologists think it may have belonged to a workshop where perfumes were made.

These painted pillars and walls were found in a villa at Pompeii.

The more lavish homes had ornately painted walls. Many of these walls survived the disaster. From them, experts know what colors Roman painters used. Scientists have even been able to analyze the paints to see how they were made.

How Did the Romans Live?

The clues found at Pompeii and Herculaneum have helped solve many mysteries about how the Romans lived.

Ancient Roman historians left detailed accounts of how the Roman Empire expanded. They also wrote about the lives of its many emperors. However, relatively few writers described the lives of ordinary Romans. They probably thought that such details were unimportant. That is why the excavation of Pompeii and Herculaneum is so revealing. The preserved remains of the two cities give a unique picture of ordinary life in 79 CE.

This mural found in Pompeii shows people buying their daily bread. →

Thanks to work at the excavation sites, experts have a good idea of how the people of both cities were living their lives on the summer day when Mount Vesuvius erupted.

Ancient Foods

Ancient food is one of the most remarkable discoveries. Archaeologists found loaves of bread being baked in ovens, meals set on dining tables in villas, cooking pots on stoves, and food for sale in the markets. From the remains of food found in the excavations at Herculaneum it is also known what people's daily diets consisted of.

ANCIENT SECRETS

Bits and Pieces

Archaeologists found **mosaics** throughout Pompeii and Herculaneum—and in the wider Roman world. They were made from tiny squares of colored glass, stone, and tile. Mosaics decorated floors and walls inside houses, and lined pools in courtyards and gardens. The most expensive mosaics showed realistic scenes or objects. Other mosiacs had abstract patterns, which were cheaper to create.

Archeologists found lentil stew, nuts, cheese, olives, eggs, and lots of bread. The richer citizens of Herculaneum also ate meat such as beef and goose, as well as fish. Such **perishable** food usually decays completely over time. At Herculaneum, it was perfectly preserved by being instantly covered and sealed by volcanic debris at very high temperatures.

This mosaic of a guard dog was intended to warn off intruders.

The same process also preserved wooden furniture at Herculaneum, although it burned humans down to the bone. At Pompeii, no skeletons or wooden items survived in the hardened ash.

A Smelly Business

Along with bread and wine, a fish sauce known as garum was another important Roman foodstuff. It was used not only for cooking but also as a form of medicine. Garum was made by putting different kinds of fish in a tank with lots of salt. It was then left to **ferment**. The tanks stank! Pompeii was one of the centers of garum production. One of the villas at Pompeii belonged to a merchant who had grown wealthy selling fish sauce. The entrance hall of his villa featured a large mosaic depicting containers of fish sauce.

This mosaic of a flask of garum from the wealthy merchant's house has a label that says "from the workshop of Scaurus."

Home Decoration

The citizens of Pompeii lived in all kinds of houses from large lavish villas to small one-room apartments. As archeologists excavated the city, they were surprised to discover that the ancient Romans loved brightly colored paints. Walls everywhere were decorated with **murals**. One of the most popular colors was bright red.

Murals in wealthy villas showed anything from Roman gods to figures from Greek myths. These murals showed other Pompeiians that the owner was cultured. In the dining room, murals were often pictures of food and drink. Pompeii's bars were decorated with images of grapes. Mosaics were also popular in homes and public buildings. Pictures had all kinds of subjects, from flowers to animals to people. One favorite type of mosaic showed a guard dog.

Writing on the Walls

Graffiti was everywhere in Pompeii. Around 6,000 pieces of graffiti have been uncovered. The word "graffiti" comes from a Latin word meaning "to scratch."

SCIENCE SOLVES IT

Puzzling Pottery

Hundreds of thousands of pieces of broken pottery have been found in the buried cities. Fitting them together is like doing thousands of jigsaw puzzles at the same time. Experts log precisely where each piece was found to try to figure out whether the different pieces might belong to the same pot. Then the pieces have to be glued together using a process of trial and error. Modern Computer-aided design now helps speed up this part of the process.

This Roman bar has paintings of grapes above the counter.

People scratched Latin words or phrases into stone surfaces using sharp needles. Some of the graffiti was very offensive. Other graffiti was about Pompeiian politics.

Life in the Town

The people who lived in Pompeii passed their time in ways that seem very familiar and modern. They went shopping seven days a week. They bought fresh and preserved food, as well as wine, spices, and olive oil. But they also bought luxury items such as silks and perfumes. These goods were transported in pottery and glass containers of various sizes.

Goods may have been stored in sacks woven from **hessian**. No one knows for sure if they were. No hessian or other forms of cloth have survived since the cities were destroyed.

While they were out shopping, Pompeiians might have visited a fast-food café, or *thermopolium*. These places were most popular with people who were too poor to have their own kitchen at home.

SCIENCE SOLVES IT

Technology to the Rescue!
In 1752 workers in Herculaneum found more than 1,800 rolled-up **papyrus** scrolls stored in a villa. When experts tried to unroll them, the papyrus crumbled. A new method proved so slow that just three scrolls were unrolled in four years! In 2005, scientists at the University of Kentucky finally came up with a way of using X-rays to read the scrolls without having to unroll them.

Elaborate murals like this were considered a sign of education.

Deep jars were sunk into a brick counter as containers for dried food such as nuts. There were jugs for water and for wine. One *thermopolium* in Pompeii was found with a kettle that was used to heat water on a fire. There were bedrooms for guests on the upper floor.

Moving Around

Like modern shoppers, Pompeiians may have suffered from traffic jams. The town was so busy that the

Tourists crowd into Pompeii's Forum in large numbers.

44

Ruts carved in the streets helped to guide cart wheels.

streets were full of carts and wagons delivering goods. The town government introduced one-way streets in an attempt to ease traffic flow. At the time, the front wheels of a cart did not turn independently of the back wheels. The wheels of all carts were a standard distance apart. In narrow streets, the authorities carved two parallel ruts in the surface of the road to guide the cartwheels. The discovery of this kind of early railroad was just one more revelation from the buried Roman cities.

Glossary

amphitheater An open building for public events, with banks of seats arranged in tiers.

aqueduct An artificial channel to carry water.

archaeology The study of the past by examining old ruins, objects, and records.

artifacts Objects made by human beings, usually with a cultural or historical value.

dormant Not active.

drones Small, uncrewed flying vehicles that are controlled remotely.

eruption A sudden and violent explosion of a volcano.

excavating Methodically uncovering and recording objects buried beneath the ground.

ferment To change state as a result of the actions of organisms such as bacteria or yeast.

forum An open place in a Roman town used as a marketplace and for public meetings.

galleries Series of covered spaces along a wall or walls.

graffiti Words or drawings written, painted, or sprayed illegally onto a wall.

hessian A rough woven textile used to make sacks or matting.

lava Hot molten or semi-molten rock that is thrown from a volcano during an eruption.

looting The stealing of goods from a place, often during a time of unrest.

methodical Carried out according to an organized system.

mosaics Pictures made of small pieces of colored stone, glass, or pottery.

murals Paintings or other works of art carried out directly on walls.

papyrus A paper-like material made from the fibers of the papyrus reed.

perishable Describes something that goes bad or rots quickly.

pumice A very light form of rock formed when volcanic lava dries.

pyroclastic flow A mass of very hot ash, lava, and gas ejected at high speed from a volcano.

radar A system of locating objects by emitting radio waves and measuring their reflection.

tsunamis Giant waves caused by earthquakes or eruptions beneath the oceans.

villas Large, luxury homes in large grounds.

Further Resources

Books

Malam, John. *You Wouldn't Want to Live in Pompeii: A Volcanic Eruption You'd Rather Avoid*. New York: Children's Press, 2008.

O'Connor, Jim. *What Was Pompeii?* What Was? New York: Turtleback, 2014.

O'Shei, Tim. *Secrets of Pompeii: Buried City of Ancient Rome*. Archeological Mysteries. North Mankato, MN: Capstone Press, 2014.

Sonneborn, Liz. *Pompeii*. Unearthing Ancient Worlds. Minneapolis: Twenty-First Century Books, 2008.

Tarshis, Lauren. *I Survived The Destruction of Pompeii, 79 A.D.* I Survived. New York: Turtleback, 2014.

Websites

www.bbc.co.uk/history/ancient/romans/pompeii_portents_01.shtml
This page from the BCC is the introduction to a series of articles for students all about Pompeii, its destruction, and its rediscovery.

www.dkfindout.com/uk/gallery/history/objects-found-at-pompeii/
Pages from Dorling Kindersley featuring a gallery of objects found at Pompeii.

www.ducksters.com/history/ancient_rome/pompeii.php
A page from the Ducksters website telling the story of Pompeii and the destruction of the Roman cities.

www.history.com/topics/ancient-history/pompeii
This page from History.com has links to many pages and videos about Pompeii and Herculaneum.

primaryfacts.com/1677/10-pompeii-facts/
The Primary Facts website has a list of 10 fascinating facts about Pompeii.

Index